William Quantrill and Quantrill's Raiders: The Confederacy's Most Notorious Bushwhackers

By Charles River Editors

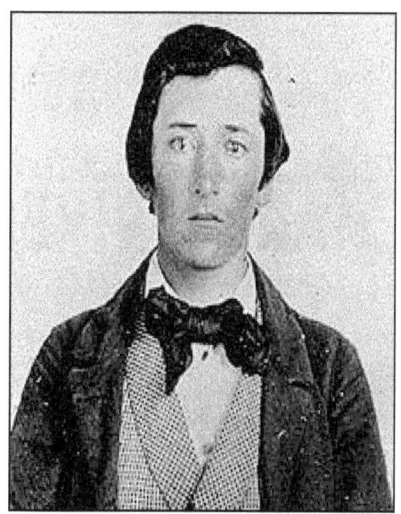

Picture of William Clarke Quantrill

About Charles River Editors

Charles River Editors provides superior editing and original writing services across the digital publishing industry, with the expertise to create digital content for publishers across a vast range of subject matter. In addition to providing original digital content for third party publishers, we also republish civilization's greatest literary works, bringing them to new generations of readers via ebooks.

Sign up here to receive updates about free books as we publish them, and visit Our Kindle Author Page to browse today's free promotions and our most recently published Kindle titles.

Introduction

William Clarke Quantrill (1837-1865)

"In all wars there have always been, and always will be a class of men designated as guerillas, but it can be said that the Missouri guerillas are more noted than those of any war in any country for ages. Their deeds of daring, their miraculous escapes, and the physical sufferings that they endured are almost beyond belief." – John McCorkle, one of Quantrill's Raiders

The Civil War is best remembered for the big battles and the legendary generals who fought on both sides, like Robert E. Lee facing off against Ulysses S. Grant in 1864. In kind, the Eastern theater has always drawn more interest and attention than the West. However, while massive armies marched around the country fighting each other, there were other small guerrilla groups that engaged in irregular warfare on the margins, and among these partisan bushwhackers, none are as infamous as William Quantrill and Quantrill's Raiders.

Quantrill's Raiders operated along the border between Missouri and Kansas, which had been the scene of partisan fighting over a decade earlier during the debate over whether Kansas and Nebraska would enter the Union as free states or slave states. In "Bloody Kansas", zealous pro-slavery and anti-slavery forces fought each other, most notably John Brown, and the region became a breeding ground for individuals like Quantrill who shifted right back into similar fighting once the Civil War started. Rather than target military infrastructure or enemy soldiers, the bushwhackers rode in smaller numbers and targeted civilians on the other side of the conflict, making legends out of men like Bloody Bill Anderson and John Mosby.

However, none are remembered like Quantrill and his men, not only because of their deeds during the Civil War but because of the actions of some of the former Raiders after it. Quantrill is best known for raiding Lawrence, Kansas in August 1863 and slaughtering nearly 200 boys and men between the ages of 14-90, under the pretext that they were capable of holding a gun and thus helping the Union cause. After that massacre, Union forces in the area retaliated in similar fashion, forcing Southern sympathizers out of several counties in the area and burning the property. Union forces also detained those accused of assisting Quantrill's Raiders, including their relatives.

After raiding Lawrence, Quantrill's Raiders headed south, and they eventually split off into several groups. Quantrill himself was killed while fighting in June 1865, nearly two months after Lee surrendered to Grant at Appomattox, but his name was kept alive by the notorious deeds of his Raiders during the war and the criminal exploits of former Raiders like Jesse James and his brother, as well as the Younger brothers. These men, who had fought with Quantrill, became some of America's most famous outlaws, and they used guerrilla tactics to rob banks and trains while eluding capture.

William Quantrill and Quantrill's Raiders: The Confederacy's Most Notorious Bushwhackers chronicles the life of Quantrill, the Raiders' Civil War record, and their legacy. Along with pictures of important people, places, and events, you will learn about Quantrill and his Raiders like never before, in no time at all.

William Quantrill and Quantrill's Raiders: The Confederacy's Most Notorious Bushwhackers

About Charles River Editors

Introduction

   Chapter 1: Bloody Kansas and Quantrill's Early Years

   Chapter 2: 1861

   Chapter 3: The Most Famous Raiders

   Chapter 4: Seasoning

   Chapter 5: 1863

   Chapter 6: The Sack of Lawrence

   Chapter 7: More Violence

   Chapter 8: Quantrill's Death

   Bibliography

Chapter 1: Bloody Kansas and Quantrill's Early Years

"[T]his momentous question, like a fire bell in the night, awakened and filled me with terror. I considered it at once as the knell of the Union. it is hushed indeed for the moment. but this is a reprieve only, not a final sentence. A geographical line, coinciding with a marked principle, moral and political, once conceived and held up to the angry passions of men, will never be obliterated; and every new irritation will mark it deeper and deeper." – Thomas Jefferson

When President Thomas Jefferson went ahead with the Louisiana Purchase, he wasn't entirely sure what was on the land he was buying, or whether the purchase was even constitutional. Ultimately, the Louisiana Purchase encompassed all or part of 15 current U.S. states and two Canadian provinces, including Arkansas, Missouri, Iowa, Oklahoma, Kansas, Nebraska, parts of Minnesota that were west of the Mississippi River, most of North Dakota, nearly all of South Dakota, northeastern New Mexico, northern Texas, the portions of Montana, Wyoming, and Colorado east of the Continental Divide, and Louisiana west of the Mississippi River, including the city of New Orleans. In addition, the Purchase contained small portions of land that would eventually become part of the Canadian provinces of Alberta and Saskatchewan. The purchase, which immediately doubled the size of the United States at the time, still comprises around 23% of current American territory.

With so much new territory to carve into states, the balance of Congressional power became a hot topic in the decade after the purchase, especially when the people of Missouri sought to be admitted to the Union in 1819 with slavery being legal in the new state. While Congress was dealing with that, Alabama was admitted in December 1819, creating an equal number of free states and slave states. Thus, allowing Missouri to enter the Union as a slave state would disrupt the balance.

The Senate ultimately got around this issue by establishing what became known as the Missouri Compromise. Legislation was passed that admitted Maine as a free state, thus balancing the number once Missouri joined as a slave state. Moreover, slavery would be excluded from the Missouri Territory north of the parallel 36°30′ north, which was the southern border of Missouri itself. As a slave state, Missouri would obviously serve as the lone exception to that line.

The Missouri Compromise of 1820 staved off the crisis for the time being, but by setting a line that excluded slave states above the parallel, it would also become incredibly contentious. Despite the attempt to settle the question with the Missouri Compromise, the young nation kept pushing further westward, and with that more territory was acquired. After the Mexican-American War ended in 1848, the sectional crisis was brewing like never before, with California and the newly-acquired Mexican territory now ready to be organized into states. The country was once again left trying to figure out how to do it without offsetting the slave-free state balance was tearing the nation apart.

With the new territory acquired in the Mexican-American War, pro and anti-slavery groups were at an impasse. The Whig Party, including a freshman Congressman named Abraham Lincoln, supported the Wilmot Proviso, which would have banned slavery in all territory acquired from Mexico, but the slave states would have none of it. Even after Texas was annexed as a slave state, the enormous new territory would doubtless contain many other new states, and the North hoped to limit slavery as much as possible in the new territories.

The Compromise of 1850 was authored by the legendary Whig politician Henry Clay. In addition to admitting California to the Union as a free state to balance with Texas, it allowed Utah and New Mexico to decide the issue of slavery on the basis of what became known as "popular sovereignty", which meant the settlers could vote on whether their state should be a free state or slave state. Though a Whig proposed popular sovereignty in 1850, popular sovereignty as an idea would come to be championed by and associated with Democratic Illinois Senator Stephen Douglas. The Compromise also abolished the slave trade – though not the existence of slavery itself – in Washington, D.C. The Whigs commended the Compromise, thinking it was a moderate, pragmatic proposal that did not decidedly extend the existence of slavery and put slow and steady limits on it. Furthermore, it made the preservation of the Union the top priority.

In an attempt to organize the center of North America – Kansas and Nebraska – without offsetting the slave-free balance, Senator Stephen Douglas of Illinois proposed the Kansas-Nebraska Act. The Kansas-Nebraska Act eliminated the Missouri Compromise line of 1820, which the Compromise of 1850 had maintained. The Missouri Compromise had stipulated that states north of the boundary line determined in that bill would be free, and that states south of it *could* have slavery. This was essential to maintaining the balance of slave and free states in the Union. The Kansas-Nebraska Act, however, ignored the line completely and proposed that all new territories be organized by popular sovereignty. Settlers could vote whether they wanted their state to be slave or free.

Stephen Douglas

When popular sovereignty became the standard in Kansas and Nebraska, the primary result was that thousands of zealous pro-slavery and anti-slavery advocates both moved to Kansas to influence the vote, creating a dangerous (and ultimately deadly) mix. Numerous attacks took place between the two sides, and many pro-slavery Missourians organized attacks on Kansas towns just across the border.

The best known abolitionist in Bleeding Kansas was a middle aged man named John Brown. A radical abolitionist, Brown organized a small band of like-minded followers and fought with the armed groups of pro-slavery men in Kansas for several months, including a notorious incident known as the Pottawatomie Massacre, in which Brown's supporters murdered five men.

Southerners in Missouri feared that free states would eventually surround the state on three sides, and the establishment of the town of Lawrence, called "Yankee town," would mean the organization of Kansas into an enemy of Missouri. Southern attempts to dictate political events in Kansas, first through voter fraud by participating in Kansas elections, and later by the intimidation and destruction of abolitionist newspapers in the territory, ensured that Northerners in Kansas would respond. Indeed, they responded in kind; "Jayhawkers" not only assaulted Southerners' homes in Kansas, they also undertook violent incursions into Missouri, operations that became much more destructive and murderous as the Civil War loomed. Jayhawkers saw their mission as one of retaliation, while the bushwhackers expressed their need for self-defense. In April 1856, there was a "border ruffian" raid on Lawrence to destroy the pro-Northern newspapers, the *Kansas Free State* and the *Herald*. The Jayhawker response was one of murderous vengeance on Southerners' properties in Kansas, leading to Brown's May 24 raid on families in the settlement near the Pottawatomie River: "Their bodies were found by kinfolk and friends in varying degrees of disfigurement -- throats cut; ears sliced off; skulls split open; bodies with multiple stab wounds; fingers, hands, or arms chopped off."[1] Over 50 people died before John Brown left the territory, which ultimately entered the Union as a free state in 1859.

John Brown

It was in this politically charged atmosphere that William Clarke Quantrill came of age in the Western states that are now considered part of the Midwest. Fittingly, young Quantrill would tell people he met that his name was Charley Hart, but the name he would ride with into battle, like the banner that said "Quantrill," was his own. This was the William Clarke Quantrill that most knew from the his self-made legends, as well as invented stories by those who lionized and demonized him. To hear them tell it, Quantrill was the son of a Ohioan school master and principal, and after he was whipped by his father in school, he would supposedly return to class trembling, his eyes alight with glimmering ferocity. He was said to torture animals and delight in the cries of their torment. A favorite of his mother, never close to his father, Quantrill was known to spend hours and hours in the woods in solitude. He had no friends and didn't appear to want any. It was these same characteristics that he would bring to his war on Kansas during the Civil War. He had no ideals, and he spoke with malice about those he contended had wronged him. And his delight in torture came with a cruel laugh that associates described as a nervous giggle.

Of course, these stories are likely apocryphal creations that tried to make sense of the man after the war. In fact, the times were filled with rumors about men, some as outrageous as any other. The Kansas colonists from New England and other Northern states were rumored to only come

---

[1] Leslie, *The Devil Knows How to Ride*, 17.

for one reason: to vote and make Kansas a free state. Other rumors filled Southerners' minds in with stories of the absence of women, for the Northern abolitionists came to transform Kansas into a replica of the free North: "Worse, it was rumored that the New England Emigrant Aide Company was sending convicts, paupers, diseased slum dwellers, viscous European immigrants, and other undesirables."[2] C.M. Chase wrote in his dispatches for the Illinois *True Republican and Sentinel*, August 10, 1862 a more articulate description of the combatants and imminent conflict: "A Jayhawker is a Unionist who professes to rob, burn out, and murder only rebels in arms against the government. A Redleg is a Jayhawker originally distinguished by the uniform of red leggings. A Redleg, however, is regarded as more purely an indiscriminate thief and murderer than the Jayhawker or Bushwhacker. A Bushwhacker is a rebel Jayhawker, or a rebel who bands with others for the purpose of preying upon the lives and property of Union citizens."[3]

In reality, Quantrill's ancestral origins suggest some kind of mental temperament that looked for adventure and thrived in periods of violence. An uncle repeatedly entered jail and abandoned wives, while Quantrill's own father fell into trouble in Canal Dover, Ohio for misappropriating school funds. When his father's public image was threatened in town, violence usually occurred, almost always leaving young William on the receiving end of a hot poker or bullwhip. Even still, his early years did not seem to hint that violence would be his profession. He succeeded nearly enough in school to become a teacher by the age of 16, but he had a strong desire to find fame and fortune with the least amount of work. If not for the death of his father, he might have ignored that impulse, but tough times for the family required him to support his mother, sister, and brothers, so Quantrill felt compelled to seek fortune in the west.

The adventurous Quantrill headed out to Mendota, Illinois at the age of 18, which was still on the edges of the frontier, and people came in the belief that with hard work, they could find success, specifically financial freedom. For Quantrill, however, it was not meant to be. He taught class again, but he was reduced to hunting and selling fowl to make ends meet. Far from finding the road to riches, Quantrill was barely making a living, and when he wrote to his mother in November 1855, he seemed to admit that his journey to the west had been in error. However, he never returned home, instead continuing to move west. The further he moved, the lonelier he got, and failure found him again and again. This forced him to move back to Ohio, as well as a rumor that he had murdered a man in Mendota. Supposedly told by the sheriff of Mendota to leave town, fear drove him home to safety. Either way, he found himself back in a classroom, facing the same prospects that compelled him to move west earlier. He could not make enough money to lift his family out of poverty, nor could he satisfy the longing in his heart for fame. Having returned to Ohio, he dwelled alone in a classroom and dreamed of something greater.

William Clarke Quantrill entered the Kansas Territory in 1857, when he was still just 19 years

---

[2] Edward E. Leslie, *The Devil Knows How to Ride: The True Story of William Clarke Quantrill and His Confederate Raiders*, 9.
[3] Leslie, *The Devil Knows How to Ride*, 29.

old. While he was there, he worked as a teacher, a successful one by the accounts of his mother and father, and he would drive cattle before moving out to Utah as a prospector. People described him as bright and eager to learn, reading voraciously (including poetry). When he entered the territory, his political views more closely followed the free soil ideas of his father, but that view changed over time, partially because he wanted to make his fortune. Politically, Quantrill's reasons to separate himself from his father's beliefs were not much different from other Ohioans. Colonists from the Midwestern states held mild anti-slavery stances, mainly due to their free soil beliefs that made no room for the presence of African Americans, whether free or slave. Even if Midwesterners did not voice free soil sentiments, their politics still held the line of a white supremacy that would make no room for blacks. The settlers only wanted uncontested land and to turn a profit from the opening of new farms. Competition with slave plantations was negotiable through violence, but in the case of Quantrill's associations with Jayhawkers, the two sides could compromise on the issue of white supremacy and the creation of profit from the sale of slaves in the rough wilderness society of Kansas.

Quantrill's shift in political views are evident in a letter dated January 26, 1860, and it is certainly ironic given how his Civil War career unfolded: "You have undoubtedly heard of the wrongs committed in this territory by the southern people, or a private party, but when one knows the facts they can easily see that it has been the opposite party that have been the main movers in the troubles & by far the most lawless set of people in the country. They all sympathize for old J. Brown, who should have been hung years ago, indeed hanging was too good for him. May I never see a more contemptible people than those who sympathize [with] him. A murderer and a robber, made a martyr of; just think of it."[4] The lesson of John Brown had not been lost on him. While he would not side with the abolitionists, he did recognize that the American public made a special place for a man who died for a cause.

Quantrill had come to the territory in the hope of gaining land to support his mother and siblings, but after two months in the wilderness full of hard work to clear land and create homesteads, Quantrill's idle ways and carefree behavioral patterns reemerged. He spent hours in the Kansas woods with a fellow idler named John Bennings, and gradually, there was little work that Quantrill would actually perform. The older men whom he had promised to work for in exchange for the defrayment of travel costs began to hound him, until Quantrill could take no more. Once again, like his ancestors, Quantrill was quick to use violence, and as with his father, he was physically humiliated, beaten by his elders within an inch of his life.

Exiled by this group of Ohioans, Quantrill sought another land claim near Tuscarora Lake among other colleagues from Canal Dover, only to get caught in the act of theft from cabins in the community. Banished again, he became a pariah, left to hunt in the woods with Jennings. A clean break with his identity and life was what he needed, and he did just that by signing on as a teamster for a U.S. Army expedition to Utah. It was here that the legend of Charley Hart was

---

[4] Leslie, *The Devil Knows How to Ride*, 62;

born, a gambler in Fort Bridger who one night lost all his winnings in one hand of cards. During this time, he wrote to his mother frequently, always with the promise that he needed more time to make his fortune honorably. This included entering the gold fields of Colorado in 1859, but he always came away with nothing. At the end of the summer of 1859, he returned to the Tuscarora Lake area and found another job as a school teacher. This would be the last peaceful time in his life, and sadness was a constant theme in his letters home. Miserably homesick, he seemed resigned to the belief that he was unable to recapture or recreate the joy of his youth: "I think everything and everybody around me is happy and I alone am miserable; it seems that man is doomed to aspire after happiness; but never in reality obtain it, for God intended the earth and not heaven for mortal man."[5] In another letter, he wrote, "I am done roving around seeking a future, for I have found [that] it may obtained being steady and industrious. And now that I have sown wild oats so long, I think it is time to begin harvesting; which will only be accomplished by putting in a different crop on a different soil."[6]

Eventually, Quantrill decided to move back home to Ohio, but along the way, he met a band of border ruffians from Missouri and his life changed dramatically. It was this fateful meeting that would help transform Quantrill into one of the country's most notorious bushwhackers and earn him a reputation as one of America's worst terrorists. Given the times he lived in, and the people who inhabited Kansas and Missouri, he might have been no worse than the murderers on both sides, but his intellect, his gift for planning, and his penchant for courage in battle would set him apart by helping him pull off one of the most devastating acts of wanton destruction in American history: the sack of Lawrence.

The way that his story has been assembled by historians might lead readers to believe that even with his change in beliefs about the conflict in Kansas, joining bands of outlaws happened accidently, as if he stumbled into the conflagration to come. There is a certain quality of uncertainty to Quantrill's life at this moment in 1860, on the cusp of the Civil War. Running into a band of bushwhackers during what might have been his departure from Kansas for Ohio, and subsequently making up his mind to join their fight, seems on the surface to be like the struggles of many young people, especially at this momentous time in history. Many young men would join the cause of the Union or the Confederacy for more intimate and personal reasons than politics, People fought for state, town, and family, and Quantrill's reason to join a bushwhacker gang might have been no different. Given his intense loneliness and battle with his perception of failure, he might have gravitated towards the bushwhackers because, having previously met them as a teamster in the U.S. Army, he felt comfortable with them. Quantrill was a man who had burned every bridge that served as a connection to his former life in Ohio, a life he thought he would never fully have again. His father had died, while the rest of his family lived in poverty. Joining the bushwhackers might have alleviated some of his mental anguish, helping him feel

---

[5] Schultz, *Quantrill's War*, 19.
[6] Leslie, *The Devil Knows How to Ride*, 61;

like he belonged. Perhaps Quantrill joined the gang simply because he was still just drifting along and not making any real decisions about his life.

Quantrill's duplicity of character, especially regarding the issue of slavery, can be understood by an examination of the dynamics between Jayhawkers and bushwhackers right before the Civil War. Quantrill's first major raid, on the plantation of the Morgan Walker, is particularly illustrative of the dynamics that produced duplicitous behaviors in all the participants of Missouri's guerrilla war. Quantrill's first brush with financial success came when he joined the bushwhackers, whose biggest source of income came from cattle theft. Cows were stolen from southern Missouri farms and sold to ranchers in Kansas, emblematic of the fact that the frontier was a bleak place to make a living and only favored the rich and the strong. The bushwhackers had learned long ago that being a border ruffian could turn a profit, including by kidnapping slaves. Kansas was filled with impoverished farms that could use a hand to break the soil and clear the land of trees, and with that, the free blacks who entered the territory became fitting targets. Moreover, the slaves of Kansas men from the South fled their masters, encouraged by Jayhawkers. The bushwhackers that Quantrill ran with got rich from kidnapping escaped slaves and free blacks.

Acts of collusion between Jayhawkers and bushwhackers were known to occur; and it was not uncommon for Quantrill, in this period before the Civil War, to associate and even ride with Jayhawkers. It worked best for both sides, as the Jayhawkers were free soil men who still believed in white supremacy and wanted Kansas free of blacks. In Quantrill's case, he actually made a profit from kidnapping slaves and free blacks at the behest of Jayhawkers, some of whom paid the gang. This act meant to clear the territory of African Americans; and the bushwhackers were free to sell the slaves to plantation owners in Missouri. It was an especially sordid type of trade, especially when Quantrill and similar bushwhackers actually coerced free blacks into giving them the location of other escaped slaves, which they then captured and sold again.

Life came together for Quantrill through his manipulation of the war between bushwhackers and Jayhawkers. During his periods of cattle rustling as a border ruffian, his quarry changed from animals to people, putting him squarely in the camp of the bushwhackers, though he still managed to ingratiate himself in with Jayhawkers. At one point, abolitionists in the area thought Quantrill was an ally, thanks to his success at stealing slaves from masters and sending them north via the Underground Railroad. Having secured the confidence of an Iowan abolitionist named John Dean, Quantrill met a party of Quaker abolitionists from Kansas intent on liberating slaves. Along with Dean and a famous Jayhawker named Eli Snyder, Quantrill planned to raid Cherokee Nation in Oklahoma and liberate slaves. Quantrill was able to convince them of another plan, a raid on the Missourian slave plantation of Andrew Walker. Here Quantrill drew up his greatest plan, contacting the eldest Walker scion with a confession of the plan and Quantrill's willingness to betray the Jayhawkers. While Walker's associates distrusted Quantrill, the Missourian lord did not. When the Jayhawkers attempted their raid, it was Quantrill who survived and almost no one else. Acceptance among the plantation families did not come instantly, but with the senior Walker's underwriting of Quantrill's pro-slavery reputation, Quantrill became a cause célèbre among the Missouri elite. He soon dressed the part of a highborn Southerner, or at least he imagined he did, decked out in a brand new denim suit. Families and friends of the Walkers entertained him in their home, and he took a Walker daughter as his mistress. Quantrill was finally a hero, at least to some.

A picture of young Quantrill

Chapter 2: 1861

By the summer of 1861, the first battles of the Civil War had begun, and the infant Confederate States of America quickly experienced its first victories. However, the new nation also realized that difficulties would beset their attempts to win victory in the Trans-Mississippi theater. The Battle of Wilson Creek and the Battle of Lexington were the biggest battles after the First Battle of Bull Run, and the Confederate victories seemed to suggest that the Confederacy would control Missouri, but overwhelming Northern strength immediately reasserted itself almost as soon as the upstart rebels sent the Union army in retreat back to the St. Louis. U.S. General John C. Fremont entered Missouri and scattered the Confederate army and pursued the remnant host into southern Missouri, eventually pushing them out of the state altogether. The effectiveness of the Confiscation Act of 1861, which allowed federal troops to confiscate any slave who labored for the Confederate military, was surpassed by Fremont's emancipation order for all slaves owned by pro-Confederates. While martial law was partially rescinded by order of President Lincoln, and the attempt at emancipation wholly abandoned, Missourians now realized that the period of Confederate ascendancy had passed.

At the same time, Kansas was in a unique political situation, as there were still two vastly different political groups residing in the region: those who meant to prevent the expansion of slavery, and others, mostly from Missouri, seeking to preserve what they saw as the right to own slaves as property. While that argument ripped the entire nation apart and led to the war, Kansas and Missouri would mostly be a battleground for guerrillas who engaged in irregular warfare and the indiscriminate murder of political opponents. Both sides, the northern "Jayhawks" and the pro-Southern "bushwhackers", would transform Missouri and Kansas into a virtual simulation of the Civil War being fought elsewhere.

When the fighting broke out between the Union and the Confederacy, new developments occurred that would make the fighting in Kansas much more violent, including the contested nature of Missouri. President Abraham Lincoln's constant shuffle of military commanders in occupied Missouri meant that Union generals were much more worried about their careers than the suppression of violence between Jayhawkers and bushwhackers, so the war between guerilla bands continued unabated despite the presence of federal forces in Missouri and Kansas. Worse, the Union army allied with Jayhawkers, while the Confederates, though defeated quickly in Missouri, aligned with the bushwhackers.

General Fremont's decree of martial-law ensured Missouri was subjected to military rule under successive Union generals, causing hardship to pro-Confederate families in the state. These families, with suspect loyalties, were forced to fund the entire cost of the occupation and war in the state, and it resulted in the loss of money and properties. All able-bodied men were ordered to join the state militia for the purposes of eradicating the southern guerrillas, even as pro-Confederate businesses, particularly newspapers, were seized. These draconian moves by the Union commanders naturally escalated the violence in Missouri, as Confederate sympathizers who had sought to make Missouri a Confederate state now had more reasons to fight the dreaded Union forces there.

Fremont

Having realized he was banished from Kansas, Quantrill stayed with his new friends the Walkers and continued to fight on the side of the self-defense forces in Missouri. The beginning of the Civil War failed to compel him to join the side of the Confederacy, but he did support the right of Southerners to own slaves. He was prepared to fight in defense of Missouri, but in the meantime, money beckoned in the form of stealing and selling of runaway slaves, which always aroused him. He traveled to Texas with runaway slaves he had captured in Texas, Kansas, and the Cherokee Nation, and he sold them to the highest bidders among the planters in Texas. These kinds of "adventures" failed to satisfy him, but not before he had made important connections, including with Cherokees who supported the Confederacy. One of the Cherokees Quantrill befriended was Chief Joel Mayes, who helped teach him guerrilla tactics and the art of ambush that had been perfected by the natives. Eventually, Quantrill enlisted to join with the Confederate army in southern Missouri.

Mayes

There were several key factors that added to the guerrilla war that overran Missouri, but the most important issue, at least on the surface, was the presence of the free state of Kansas as a base for continued raids by Jayhawkers.[7] Before and after Union forces officially occupied the state, bands of committed Jayhawkers attacked southern Missouri in support of the invasion of the Union army from the North. Along with other slave plantations, the Walker plantation that Quantrill was so fond of was forced to defend itself, doing so through the Blue Springs self-defense militia.

In the first months of the war, Quantrill, along with bushwhackers and Cherokees, acted as a reserve cavalry that hung back while the regular Confederate army fought the major battles. While Quantrill was technically a Confederate soldier at this point, and he fought bravely when called on to confront Union soldiers, he preferred to stay on the margins of the battle in order to plunder the battlefield. Quick riches still suited his taste, while marching to battle did not and never could.

In time, Walker's self-defense militia became Quantrill's own, and in "Quantrill Country," the western Missourian terrain characterized by flat open land dotted with woods that irregulars could dash into, the population of Missouri took care of Quantrill and other bushwhackers.

---

[7] *The Second Major Battle of the Civil War*, Wilsons Creek National Battlefield, National Park Service, http://www.nps.gov/wicr/index.htm

Citizens fed, housed, and supplied the guerrillas, and when Union troops failed to penetrate the wilderness havens of the bushwhackers, Quantrill and the other bushwhackers emerged and sought shelter with the populace. The visits were frequent and took, on the surface, the appearance of many liberties with the citizenry's property. On closer inspection, however, citizens appeared to recount the episodes with pride and nostalgia. One citizen recalled the stories their grandfather told about the war: "[H]e would wake up in the night and see somebody in front of the fireplace taking off his boots. The, walking in his sock feet, the person would go into a room that was seldom used and go to bed. Sometime the outside door would be silently opened and clothes put inside the house. This was a sign they needed to be mended; and this my grandmother would do, and in a few days someone would call for them. Sometimes, when my grandfather went to the stable in the morning, he would find one of his horses gone and a strange one in its stall, usually lame, or one that had lost a shoe. As soon as the lameness was gone, my grandfather would replace the shoe. In a few days he would go again to the stable and there would be his own horse, and the other would be gone. This is the way our people helped each other."[8]

Another important step taken by the Confederates in 1861 was the Partisan Ranger Act of 1861, which made no distinction between "partisans" and "guerrillas". In short, both groups were to report to Confederate armies and be integrated into their commands for operations, but the irregulars were expected to live behind enemy lines and switch between civilian clothes and military uniforms. Quantrill himself would hold a commission within the Confederate army but act independently. While the Partisan Ranger Act of 1861 means the establishment of these bushwhacker units can at least be partly blamed on the Confederate government, they were powerless to control Quantrill's Raiders. One of Quantrill's chief lieutenants, "Bloody Bill" Anderson, later said "I don't care any more than you for the South...but there is lot of money in this [bushwhacking] business."[9]

Chapter 3: The Most Famous Raiders

Quantrill's Raiders could be categorically defined as men fighting for the Confederacy, states' rights, and slavery, but in most cases, the men actually saw the war as an opportunity to reinvent and enrich themselves. By the end of the war, the last of their numbers were mostly rogues who had found another way to occupy their libertine times. Vengeance against the Northern invaders unified them, and they chose violence as their medium of expression. Soldiering did not satiate the desire for bloodshed, but raiding and ambushing did.[10]

One of Quantrill's most important associates was "Bloody Bill" Anderson, who made a knot in a silken rope for every man he killed. By the time he was killed in battle in late 1864, his rope

---

[8] Schultz, *Quantrill's War*, 81-82.
[9] Geiger, *Financial Fraud and Guerrilla Violence*, 104-105.
[10] William Pennington, "Roster of Quantrill's, Anderson's, and Todd's Guerrillas, and other 'Missouri Jewels,'" http://penningtons.tripod.com/roster.htm

had 54 knots. Anderson came from a family infamous for their predations on the Kansas prairies, specifically the Santa Fe Trail, and his father was shot dead by a judge over a stolen horse. With the law ready to throw Bill in jail, the family left for Missouri, where the hard life as a pirate of the plains made Anderson a tough man who colleagues said loved to kill. According to contemporaries, the act of violence provoked him to froth at the mouth, and he never spared a man's life.

Bloody Bill Anderson

Along with Anderson, handsome features also described George Todd, a Canadian whose love of killing was his most known characteristic. While Anderson was known for his long ringlets of black hair, Todd's blue eyes and blond hair made him stand out. Like Anderson, good looks contradicted his sinister deposition. Unlike Anderson's bloodthirsty familial ties, nothing seemed to suggest why Todd chose the life of a bushwhacker, but a partial explanation seemed to come in his young age during the move to Missouri. By the age of 18, his experiences on the frontier had led him to a life of theft and murder. Quantrill would rely on him more than other guerrilla, and eventually, he would rival Quantrill for leadership.

Frank and Jesse James hailed from Missouri, and Frank was a prisoner at the Battle of Wilson's Creek. He joined Quantrill's outfit because he was on parole as a former prisoner, and no Confederate unit would accept parolees. His younger brother Jesse stayed on at the family farm until Union militia seized him at his farm and pistol-whipped him nearly to death before throwing him in a cornfield. When he came back to his home, his stepfather had been hung to die, and his mother and sister were thoroughly terrified. Jesse joined Quantrill because his brother belonged to the guerrilla fighters too.

Jesse James

Jesse and Frank James

Thomas Coleman Younger, known as Cole Younger, came from a Missourian family like Jesse and Frank James. However, unlike the James brothers, Younger lived an easy life as the son of successful plantation and farm owner. His father never preached secession, but the depredations of Jayhawkers and their destruction of farm properties helped make up the patriarch's mind to support for the Confederacy. The family ran afoul of Union army occupiers who targeted Cole for his suspected rebel support, and a later Union raid against the Younger estates left Cole's father dead and his corpse robbed, provoking Cole to join Quantrill intent on revenge. However, Cole also exhibited an idealism that separated him from the other guerillas, and he provided mercy to people during the war when even Quantrill did not.

Chapter 4: Seasoning

Whether the superior horsemen of Quantrill's Raiders deceptively wore Union blue or announced their southern pride with the bushwhacker's "red vest," the guerrillas suffered hard lessons during their near-annihilation at the hands of federal forces before scoring two major victories that demonstrated Quantrill's leadership skills and the abilities of his partisans. These episodes demonstrated that no matter Quantrill's martial abilities and courage, he still needed experience to make correct decisions against an experienced foe that followed traditional military tactics. Moreover, there were no illusions regarding their brand of warfare; Quantrill's Raiders knew that the Union army and supporting militias would execute any captured guerrillas. In fact, it may have been U.S. General Henry Halleck's general order to not treat partisans as prisoners-of-war that influenced Quantrill's Raiders and their decisions to abandon any decorum of war. The threat of execution without standard military protections may have led them to believe it was only fair to fight according to their own philosophy, one that replaced honor with brutality.

What is certain was Quantrill's flair for the dramatic, which apparently included drawing a line in the dirt in front of his men. After he read Halleck's proclamation, Quantrill gave them a decision: either continue to fight and face certain death, or go home now. Quantrill, of course, chose to keep fighting, and the men who crossed the line did more than follow him into battle; they unwittingly participated in a trial-by-fire of Quantrill's military skills.

Union soldiers from Kansas and Missouri soon gave chase to Quantrill's Raiders, and on at least three different occasions, the Missourian bushwhackers were surrounded by federals. At Little Santa Fe, the sentries he posted fell asleep and allowed the 2nd Kansas Volunteers to set fire to the house where they were staying. Only Quantrill's calm command allowed them to escape. In lower Jackson County, in the Pink Hill area, the 1st Missouri Cavalry caught up with the guerrillas, cut them off from their horses, and forced them to abandon their mounts and run away on foot. At the Lowe farm, 12 miles southwest of Independence, the 7th Missouri Infantry surprised Quantrill by marching in a thunderous rainstorm and forcing them, once again, to abandon their horses and hide in the woods.

On each occasion, they lived to fight another day, but the significance of the near-disasters was not lost on the members of Quantrill's band. William Gregg remarked in his unpublished memoir on Quantrill's early command: "The ambushes at the Tate, Clark, and Lowe farms taught him the absolute necessity of always putting out pickets and of using for the detail only the most stalwart and reliable men. He also began to choose his camping sites with an eye to defense against ambush. The lessons were valuable beyond eliminating the tiresome and frequent necessity of replacing all the horses."[11]

After repeated chances to catch Quantrill his men, frustration must have set in for the federals. Word reached Major James O. Gower of guerrilla activity, and he sent the 1st Iowa Cavalry on a midnight march towards Sugar Creek near Wadesburg. The vanguard, patrols Gower sent out, soon located Quantrill's men drying out their blankets and coats. This time, however, the guerrillas stood ready. Quantrill stationed pickets outside the farm to prevent a surprise attack, and an overeager patrol stormed towards the rebel camp. Quantrill had waited for this moment, figuring it was just a matter of time before a Union cavalry unit would overpursue and run

---

[11] Leslie, *The Devil Knows How to Ride*, 163.

straight into his maximum firepower. The guns of his men achieved this objective, sending concentrated volleys into the heart of the charge of the horsemen. Mounts and soldiers collapsed, and the Union cavalry withered in the storm of buckshot and raced back to cover. Quantrill's men rounded up the riderless horses and stripped the dead from their saddles, also taking guns, ammunition, and canteens of whiskey.

    Quantrill used a spyglass to observe the beaten-back cavalry's position, rightly figuring that their refusal to fully retreat probably meant a larger Union force was in the vicinity. He soon saw a dust cloud indicating he was right, and yet again Quantrill realized he was faced with the possibility of total annihilation. A ravine was located behind the house, a perfect place to make one more stand before a retreat into the woods. When the 1st Iowa Cavalry came on for another charge, guerilla fusillades beat them back. The guerillas now had time to leap into the ravine and grab the horses, but unexpectedly, the Union forces did not let the five foot drop of the ravine deter them. They rushed wildly into the rebels' position, first firing rifles, then their sidearms, and then swinging rifles and slashing with knives. The intensity of the hand-to-hand combat forced the bushwhackers to recoil, and they quickly beat a retreat and disappeared into the woods.

    On the surface, the battle looked like a Union victory, but Quantrill proved his forces could stand toe-to-toe with a federal unit, inflict damage on them, and retreat. This instilled confidence in Quantrill and his men, who were now bolder when it came to their ranging operations. He did not intend to pick future engagements with Union soldiers in the open, but his men could still slug it out in a traditional military way when necessary.

A picture of some of Quantrill's Raiders

Still, Quantrill viewed the retreat as another defeat, and he spoiled for another chance to upend the federal occupation of Missouri. He was not the only Confederate spoiling for a fight. Colonel Hughes wanted to recruit more Missourians into the Confederate army in Arkansas, which lay in wait to return to their home state, and he called upon Quantrill to serve as his auxiliary force. Along with his own 25 men and Colonel Hayes' 300 green recruits, now Hughes possessed 400.

The target chosen was Independence, Missouri. Hughes believed that if the outpost could be destroyed, if not captured, then the act would lift Southern morale and allow Hughes to continue his recruitment drive in the north. The commander of the Union garrison at Independence was Colonel Buel, who had under his command 300 federal soldiers. He never realized what the Confederate raiders meant to attack, so he left his soldiers in indefensible positions, with the main force in an open tent city a half mile west of the city. More crucially, Buel lived in a separate house, housing his command in a position that isolated him from the rest of his army.

When the Confederate raiders attacked, they did not know about the federals' unpreparedness for battle. Quantrill successfully led his 25 raiders into Independence with the intention to surround Buel, separate him from his command, and kill him. They succeeded in all their objectives save one: murdering the Union commander. Having trapped him in the house, they started a fire, saying "Surrender or roast." Buel yelled out the window and asked for treatment as a prisoner-of-war.

John McCorkle recalled the actions of Quantrill's Raiders in Independence in his book *Three Years With Quantrill*:

> "During this time, Quantrell, who had been pursuing the Federals toward Kansas City returned and, dashing up into the town, began to fire at the windows of the court house and bank building. Discovering that he was unable to dislodge the Federals, called for volunteers to rush in and set fire to the bank building. Cole Younger and my brother volunteered, and, rushing to a nearby carpenter shop, they gathered an armful of shavings each, Cole going to the front door, and my brother to the rear door, and, piling the shavings against the doors, set fire to them. The men, in the meantime, kept a constant fire at the windows. As soon as the smoke began to rise, the Federals ran out a white flag and said they would surrender if they would be treated as prisoners of war, afterwards saying that they would have surrendered before, but knowing it was Quantrell and his men, they were afraid. They were assured that they would be treated as prisoners of war and were drawn up in line on the courthouse square and disarmed and were paroled and let go free.
>
> When we first entered Independence, there were confined in the county jail two Southern men, Frank Harbaugh and Bill Bassham, who had been sentenced by the Federal officers to be shot the next day. Neither of these men had ever taken any part in the war, Harbaugh being a farmer and Bassham in the employ of the Government, carrying the overland mail. As soon as we had entered the town, George Todd took ten men with him and went to the jail and, securing sledge hammers from a blacksmith shop, broke the doors in and released these two men. As soon as they were free, Bassham began calling for a gun and was told to go to the provost-marshal's office, which was filled with guns that had been taken from the Southern citizens. He rushed to die office, secured him a double-barrelled shot gun, and immediately began to try to get even with the men that had put him in jail, but Harbaugh didn't seem to desire any gun, but started for home on a dead run and I have never seen nor heard of him since, but suppose he has stopped running ere this. Among the men captured by us was a neighbor boy of mine, Anderson Cowgill, whom I had known for years and after he was paroled, I went up to him and offered to speak to him, but he refused, saying, 'I will get even with you yet,'..."

Thus, the surrender request, despite Quantrill's vehemence about Halleck's "extermination" order, was granted to the U.S. soldiers. The Union army laid down their weapons and finally surrendered, becoming prisoners who were summarily paroled. Mercy was worth the fruits of the attack and occupation of Independence, and the aftermath of the battle resulted in the type of result that the Confederates had desired. Morale was significantly raised in the South.

While not much is known about the majority of Quantrill's actions in early 1863, the most significant event to take place was a love affair. Sarah "Kate" King came from the Robert King family nearby Blue Springs, and there is much disagreement regarding her age when she met Quantrill. While Kate wrote little about their first meeting, her age has been approximated between 13-15 years old. Quantrill was known to have appreciated her good riding skills and quick wit; but Kate also was legendary as a buxom girl with a sturdy figure. The courtship period lasted a few months, which saw their riding adventures turn into long talks on the King property. Eventually her father disapproved of their meetings, no doubt due to Quantrill's murderous notoriety and her young age, but their courtship took on a more forbidding love type of quality, and rumors attempted to do more than suggest that Quantrill kidnapped Kate. His force of matrimonial vows was another story, but evidence does not exist to prove either rumor. In the later part of her life, she did speak lovingly of her brief relationship with Quantrill; in fact, Kate appeared to have created if not preserved a pleasant memory of the rebel guerrilla, the husband from her childhood.

Meanwhile, the victory at Independence did not change Quantrill's preference for guerrilla war, along with murder and destruction. His tactics still exhibited qualities of the need for retribution; when news reached him of the execution of Perry Hoy, an esteemed Missourian bushwhacker, Quantrill responded with his own act of vengeance, executing a Union captive. At the same time, he still behaved in compliance with his rank of a captain and as a commissioned officer in the Confederate army, which was formally granted to him on August 1862. When Confederate armies required his support for attacks on Union positions, he obeyed and responded in kind. However, he displayed a distaste for Confederate regulars, partly for his belief that some commanders did not fully respect the lives of his men and intended to use them arbitrarily in battle with little thought of their destruction.

Of course, a more likely explanation could be Quantrill's dislike for the nature of battle that traditional warfare demanded. This did not suit his style of fighting, as it did not really allow for raids on supply wagons and executions of militiamen, not to mention the destruction of homes and other properties. Missouri continued to suffer from his raids, done partly as acts of reprisal, and partly to destroy pro-Union militias and the families that supported federals. His way of war meant that Missouri slowly settled into a type of society that could barely support the homes in the rural quarters; and Missourians knew this. More and more families on both sides alike began to leave the state, as did Quantrill when winter set in. Quantrill moved most of his men, at this point unofficially 200, to winter quarters in Arkansas, and there was no reason to think he would change the ways that established his success in 1862.

Chapter 5: 1863

The first half of 1863 saw Quantrill's melt back into the woods and swell with new recruits. Much of the reason lay with the seasons. Men in smaller numbers could handle winter quarters better than big groups, and occasionally, the presence of Confederate soldiers necessitated the support of guerillas as scouts. For example, Quantrill's Raiders served as scouts for Joe Shelby's Missouri "Iron" Brigade during Shelby's time on the Missouri-Arkansas border, and the bushwhackers fought in a few small battles in the Trans-Mississippi theater. That said, many raiders left the field of battle, demonstrating their distaste for organized military life, and some of them even left Quantrill's command to head home to Missouri. This fluidity of membership, with some guerrillas going home while others fought in smaller bands, is not only partly explained by the pull of home but also the conditions of the war in the Trans-Mississippi. Bushwhackers, Jayhawkers, "red legs," and militias rampaged around the Kansas and Missouri border, and all parties were affected, pro-Union and pro-Confederate alike. Neither side even attempted to determine the allegiance of some who were caught up in their raids, ensuring that lives and properties were all destroyed.

Quantrill's men not only left to avenge the destruction of their family's homes, they also launched raids deep into Kansas, and there was very little the Union army and militias could do. Federal attention focused on the Jayhawkers, who many Missourians, though Unionist in sentiment, blamed for the acts of violence carried out by vengeful bushwhackers, but Kansas also began to beckon to bushwhackers because the state wasn't as war torn as Missouri. Farms were ripe with horses, food, and other supplies ready for the taking, and the Union recognized that raiders were regularly peeling off from larger units to attack Kansas, so military command divided the District of Kansas into the "District of the Border" and the "District of the Frontier." The designation did little to change the nature of war; it merely made the Union army more distrustful of Missourians and Kansans.

Chapter 6: The Sack of Lawrence

Some historians believe that Quantrill had lost control over his raiders by the summer of 1863, because while he made small raids during this time, he apparently preferred sitting in a cabin with Kate, perhaps even retiring from the war. Eventually, however, things changed in Missouri that compelled him to take action ad reclaim his mantle of leadership in the process. The policy of the Union army in the District of the Border was to destroy the ability of the pro-Southern families to support the guerrillas, so Union forces targeted and arrested the families in the region, for the purpose of exile and relocation out of Missouri. The temporary jail for suspected rebel families was housed in Kansas City, which included many women and young children. Overpacked into the cells, the old building turned into a deathtrap, culminating in the collapse of the building on August 13, 1863. The walls fell down and the roof collapsed, killing four women and permanently maiming 11 others. Two of the women were sisters of Bloody Bill Anderson, and Cole Younger also lost a cousin in the collapse. Anderson and Younger, along with many other Missourians, never forgave what they perceived as a disregard for the safety of women in the prison by the federal army, and the tragedy in Kansas City would be used by members of Quantrill's Raiders and other bushwhackers to justify their destruction of Lawrence.[12]

The willingness of Quantrill's Raiders to conduct the risky raid, especially after many of them had continued their partisan activities without Quantrill's leadership, was not a foregone conclusion. Quantrill had to exercise considerable capital with his Confederate rank and popularity, and he knew that if he could not convince them to attack Lawrence now, he might never have had the chance again. His lieutenants - Anderson, Todd, Greg, Cole Younger, and Yeager - unanimously agreed to destroy Lawrence and kill every male in the town.

The collapse of the Kansas City jail is often cited as the motive that compelled the raid on Lawrence, but the fact is that the jail's collapse occurred three days after the vote to raid Lawrence. Thus, a better explanation for the attack on Kansas can be found merely in the frustrations of pro-Southern bushwhackers. The Union was winning the Civil War in the Western theater, and the Trans-Mississippi looked to fall soon after. If it was not the supremacy of the Northern arms and men, then the reason for frustration came with the relentless fury of Jayhawkers and red-legs, who continued to target Confederate sympathizers with impunity. For his part, Quantrill claimed he would "plunder, and destroy the town in retaliation for Osceola", a Union attack that had taken place back in September 1861.

After safely reconnoitering Lawrence and penning a death list of Lawrence abolitionists, Quantrill brought his band to the Kansas line, and along the way, more Confederate army recruits joined his numbers. By the time the march began, 450 riders plunged into the thick brush of the Kansas plains. McCorkle recalled, "On the morning of the 20th of August, Quantrell gave the order to break camp and march in a southwesterly direction, and went over on the Big Blue to a point south of Little Santa Fe, a town just on the Kansas line. His entire march until he reached the Kansas line was through smoking ruins and blackened fields. He halted in the woods all day and just about dark he gave the order to mount and crossed into Kansas at a point about ten miles south of Little Santa Fe and turned directly west toward the town of Lawrence, and, riding all night, the town was reached just at daylight."

The rapid killing to come in Lawrence does not adequately explain the trouble that Quantrill had leading his band deep into Kansas, nor does it touch on the heroism of the residents of Lawrence who nearly stopped Quantrill before he arrived in the town and tried to put up a defense when they did. The size of Quantrill's force, nearly 450 men, boggled the mind and may have been the biggest guerilla attack of the Civil War. A force this large, cutting a swath some 40 feet across the plains, could not cross into Kansas undetected. At numerous times along the way,

---

[12] Thomas Goodrich, *Bloody Dawn: The Story of the Lawrence Massacre*, 9; National Park Service, "The Second Major Battle of the Civil War," Wilson Creek National Battlefield, http://www.nps.gov/wicr/index.htm

civilians in homesteads did witness the ride of the raiders, but these people could only wonder if the men they saw in Union blue were federal troops or disguised bushwhackers. Plenty of chances remained for people to warn western Kansas; for many thought there could be but one place this suspicious force meant to attack: Lawrence. Rumors existed in the days leading up to the sack that Quantrill intended to attack on the next full moon, but that didn't come to pass, because Quantrill meant to cross in total darkness, knowing if a full moon illuminated his force, the attack would fail.

Union Captains Coleman and Pike had heard that a large force of guerrillas had entered the state, in all likelihood ready to strike Lawrence, and the Union army and associated militias were able to marshal their forces and give chase to the rebels. However, they proved unable to track the guerrillas because Quantrill and his lieutenants took advantage of the greatest strength of the bushwhackers: the ability to split up into separate bands and arrive at a rendezvous spot. While outnumbered, the raiders outsmarted the federals and arrived to a town that thought itself vulnerable but also defensible.[13]

Another reason the Missouri bushwhackers were not stopped before Lawrence was because there were Union forces in Lawrence. In fact, a newspaper in Lawrence had claimed a few weeks earlier, "Lawrence has ready for any emergency over five hundred fighting men...every one of who would like to see [Quantrill's raiders]." However, they were never alerted or put in a position that could have allowed them to counterattack. The town's militia would be no match for Quantrill's Raiders, but the Union army in the region (nearly 10,000 strong) and the acting auxiliary militias could have prevented the disaster at Lawrence. The failure to stop the disaster can be explained by bad luck and lack of preparations, but Quantrill was also undertaking an operation no one thought possible.

August 20, 1863 was a moonless night, and Quantrill meant to strike quickly, but he also urged caution, not wanting the band to separate before reaching Lawrence in full strength. Some bands rode ahead as scouts in case the Union army did stake out pickets outside the town, and Todd particularly relished his role as a harbinger of death and destruction. He attacked farms and killed men where they stood, while Quantrill ordered the imprisonment of men who knew the way to Lawrence. Quantrill and his lieutenants were familiar with the trail, but they were worried that settlers would see them and rush off to warn Lawrence.

Eventually, they met at the rendezvous spot and assembled for the raid, looking at the town from a ridge. Quantrill sent his lieutenants out with copies of the death list, after which bands broke up and rode into the margins of town. Some voiced their last doubts again, and whether or not they should turn back, so Quantrill declared one last time that anyone who wanted to go home still could.

---

[13] Goodrich, *Bloody Dawn: The Story of the Lawrence Massacre*

As the bands began riding toward Lawrence, the town had no clue what was coming. Farmers on the edge of town were the first to die, shot down as they did their morning chores, and from there, the killings accelerated. On the outskirts of Lawrence, McCorkle remembered, "At the entrance to the town, there were a lot of tents in which were camped a detachment of negro soldiers and a few white men. The command halted here and someone fired a shot. Immediately the negroes and white men rushed out of their tents, the majority of them starting in the direction of the river and some going in the direction of town. The command was given to break ranks, scatter and follow them. A few of the negroes reached the river, plunging into it, but none succeeded in reaching the opposite shore. The troops then dashed back up into the town, down the main street, shooting at every blue coat that came in sight. Just before entering the town Colonel Quantrell turned to his men and said, 'Boys, this is the home of Jim Lane and Jennison; remember that in hunting us they gave no quarter. Shoot every soldier you see, but in no way harm a woman or a child.' He dashed ahead of his command down Main Street, firing his pistol twice, dismounted from his horse and went into the hotel, where he was met by the landlord, whom he recognized as an old friend and immediately gave orders for the landlord not to be molested and stayed in the hotel and guarded him. During all this time, his command were busy hunting men with blue clothes and setting fire to the town."

People slowly came out of their homes, only to find that Quantrill's vanguard was swift. Men were shot where they stood in their doorjambs, while others found guns pressed to their faces, told to help the raiders find the residences of people on the death list. Most obeyed, only to watch torches put to their houses. As more and more people began to rise from their homes and determine the cause of the sporadic gunfire, a thunderous avalanche of horse hooves descended on downtown, riding right down the main street, Massachusetts Street. By now, the gunfire became more intense, and whoops of celebration echoed in the streets of Lawrence. A lone gong sounded as a warning to the invasion, and with that, fires began to rage everywhere. One writer described the scene, "And the day was actually darker than it had begun. Burning homes and barns sent spires of smoke upward until they converges to form a huge pall over the city, blotting out the sun and sky. Massachusetts Street was a raging wall of flame and churning black clouds. Crunching timber and toppling bricks fed the roar, and the heat was so intense that no one dared enter the street. Even the sidewalks were burning. And everywhere was the suffocating dark fog. Women, some carrying babies in their arms, ran through the streets shielding their faces from the fire, crying and screaming for husbands and sons."[14]

While Quantrill fancied himself a soldier, his assault on Lawrence was anything but a military battle, and within the first hours of the sack, the raiders behaved just like party-goers who did not want to cease their celebrations. Although the raid on Lawrence had specific objectives, the discipline among Quantrill's Raiders inevitably began to break down. While bands led by Bloody Bill Anderson and Todd engaged in indiscriminate murder, other raiders intended to

---

[14] Goodrich, *Bloody Dawn*, 118.

pillage the town for guns and liquor. Others were looking to steal horses and anything else they could use for making war. Quick work was made of the men who could fight, who were armed, and who posed a threat; the Union army barracks that still contained soldiers were mercilessly gutted by the raiders. Tents were knocked over, horses trampled over men still asleep, and others were shot. As the raiders descended on individual farms and homes, men were quickly led out of their houses at gunpoint.

By this time, most Lawrence inhabitants could read the writing on the wall. Some men begged for mercy and others tried to run, only to be shot down or executed in cold blood. Other husbands told their sons to run off so they could reason with the raiders, knowing full well that all they could ask was that the women and children be spared. One woman recalled a few weeks after the attack, "My father was very slow to get into the cornfield. He was so indignant at the ruffians that he was unwilling to retreat before them. My little children were in the field three hours. They seemed to know that if they cried the noise would betray their parents whereabouts, & so they kept as still as mice. The baby was very hungry & I gave her an ear of raw green corn which she ate ravenously." The raiders mostly obliged requests to spare women and children, but that decorum did not extend to their houses. Many families would have to spend the winter homeless.

Harper's Weekly illustration depicting the ruins of Lawrence

If any heroes existed in Lawrence, it was the women. With Quantrill's orders to "kill every man big enough to carry a gun," a lot of the men ran, even without knowing anything about the "death lists." The men who fled from their families looked for the most impregnable buildings, while others ran to the cornfields. Many wanted to stay and defend their homes from attack, but the women who understood the futility of putting up resistance pleaded with them to run. When the raiders came into their houses, the women were helpless to stop the plunder and burning, but they managed to save their children, even while they watched the slaughter of their husbands, fathers, sons, and brothers. Some even managed to save their homes, braving the bullets and knives of bushwhackers to put out the fires. When Lawrence was rebuilt, the women preserved the first bricks, but the town would be short many of its men.

While the people of Lawrence were caught unawares and suffered the most, some of the townspeople and nearby Union forces tried to offer up some resistance near the town. Led by Senator Jim Lane, whose name was on the "death lists", the Lawrencians could only muster up some old mules and the tired horses of the raiders. Along with the antique weapons they carried, including muskets, squirrel rifles, pepper-box pistols, they began to fall helplessly behind but still managed to keep sight of the main host. Major Plumb's cavalry also bore down on the guerrillas, but rebel arms repeatedly prevented any concerted federal attack from stalling the escape.

Eventually, more Union soldiers headed to Lawrence to try to deal with Quantrill's Raiders. McCorkle described the chaos, "Quantrell and his command had come to Lawrence to be avenged and they were. In this raid, a few innocent men may have been killed but this was not intentional. As the command left the town, they discovered a command of Federals coming in pursuit. The whole face of the earth looked blue. One of Quantrell's men returned to the town and was literally riddled with bullets. The command then turned south, with the Federals still in close pursuit and having gone about two miles, stopped at a big house. There was no one at home, but the doors were open and one of the rooms was fitted up as a doctor's office, a lot of bottles and medicine setting on the shelves. The boys knocked the medicine all down and soon the house was afire, a case of spontaneous combustion. Tom Hamilton and another one of boys were wounded in Lawrence; they were placed in as ambulance and brought to the command. These were placed with the advance guard of twenty men under Dick Yeager, who was appointed to pilot the command out. Before the horses had finished eating, the pickets fired; the order was given to mount and go west through a lane, the Federals getting closer all the time."

Quantrill and his force neared the Missouri border, seemingly home free as an intact guerrilla unit, but more Union pursuers stepped into their path towards Missouri, momentarily holding them in town after town. These men were led by Captains Coleman and Pike, who previously tried in vain to intercept them before Lawrence. The bushwhackers continued to run into federals and militia, usually in the form of forward cavalry units that attempted to ambush the guerrillas. The arrival of enemies from the north, eager to outflank, forced them to attempt shortcuts across farms they knew nothing about. Now slowed down in terrain they barely knew and bottled up on old country roads and dense forests, the arrival of hundreds of Kansas farmers, alerted by the destruction of Lawrence, threatened to envelop and destroy the guerrillas. Quantrill was forced to break up his force into smaller bands and head for Missouri. Only the total disorganization of the pursuers allowed the core of Quantrill and his raiders to escape the state.

Chapter 7: More Violence

Naturally, the violence in Lawrence begot more violence as pro-Union guerrillas vowed revenge. A long period of killing engulfed the Missouri and Kansas borderlands; and bloodshed would not stop even with the cessation of hostilities at the end of the Civil War. Frustrated by their failure to capture the bushwhackers, and knowing that guerrillas still lurked in the farmlands of eastern Kansas, the Jayhawkers, the red legs, and the militias acted on the orders of the Union command in Kansas City to kill all suspected bushwhackers in the countryside. The murders intensified, and many strangers were gunned down or hung on the spot. In the aftermath of the notorious raid, one Kansas abolitionist described the impact of the raid and tied it to the endless cycle of violence: "Viewed in any light, the Lawrence Raid will continue to be held, as the most infamous event of the uncivil war! The work of destruction did not stop in Kansas. The cowardly criminality of this spiteful reciprocity lay in the fact that each party knew, but did not care, that the consequences of their violent acts would fall most heavily upon their own helpless friends. Jenison in 1861 rushed into Missouri when there was no one to resist, and robbed and killed and sneaked away with his spoils and left the union people of Missouri to bear the vengeance of his crimes. Quantrell in 1863 rushed into Lawrence, Kansas, when there was no danger, and killed and robbed and sneaked off with his spoils, leaving helpless women and children of his own side to bear the dreadful vengeance invoked by that raid. So the Lawrence raid was followed by swift and cruel retribution, falling, as usual in this border warfare, upon the innocent and helpless, rather than the guilty ones. Quantrell left Kansas with the loss of one man. The Kansas troops followed him, at a respectful distance, and visited dire vengeance on all western Missouri. Unarmed old men and boys were accused and shot down, and homes with their now meagre comforts were burned, and helpless women and children turned out with no provision for the approaching winter. The number of those killed was never reported, as they were scattered all over western Missouri."

Quantrill and his band had succeeded beyond expectations, and because of it, the Union army in Missouri was forced to do something about the bushwhackers. The debacle at Lawrence was the type of disaster that made men lose jobs; and General Thomas Ewing, Jr., as commander of the District of the Border, looked to catch the most blame. He was left with no alternative but to issue General Order No. 11. Senator Lane drafted the order, perhaps even adding more punitive terms to its language, and it was a legal document like few others in American history.

"General Order No. 11.

Headquarters District of the Border,

Kansas City, August 25, 1863.

1. All persons living in Jackson, Cass, and Bates counties, Missouri, and in that part of Vernon included in this district, except those living within one mile of the limits of Independence, Hickman's Mills, Pleasant Hill, and Harrisonville, and except those in that part of Kaw Township, Jackson County, north of Brush Creek and west of Big Blue, are hereby ordered to remove from their present places of residence within fifteen days from the date hereof.

Those who within that time establish their loyalty to the satisfaction of the commanding officer of the military station near their present place of residence will receive from him a certificate stating the fact of their loyalty, and the names of the witnesses by whom it can be shown. All who receive such certificates will be permitted to remove to any military station in this district, or to any part of the State of Kansas, except the counties of the eastern border of the State. All others shall remove out of the district. Officers commanding companies and detachments serving in the counties named will see that this paragraph is promptly obeyed.

2. All grain and hay in the field or under shelter, in the district from which inhabitants are required to remove, within reach of military stations after the 9th day of September next, will be taken to such stations and turned over to the proper officers there and report of the amount so turned over made to district headquarters, specifying the names of all loyal owners and amount of such product taken from them. All grain and hay found in such district after the 9th day of September next, not convenient to such stations, will be destroyed."

In essence, the orders gave the Union army the power to evict thousands of families from Missouri and break the back of the slave-holding system in Missouri. Ewing had refused to issue the plan before, but after Lawrence, he couldn't hold back; as Lane explained, he would be a dead dog if he did not implement the orders. Naturally, it would end up being the most controversial act of Ewing's career, but with that, Kansas and Missouri had taken another step towards total war. As one writer put it, "The orders led to the ruin of thousands of lives and created a wasteland eighty-five miles long and fifty miles wide, from the Missouri River in the north to the Osage river in the south. General Orders 11 decreed that everyone living within those boundaries had to leave the area within fifteen days. The only exceptions permitted were homes located within one mile of a town in which Union troops were stationed and whose residents could prove their loyalty to the Union cause. Not many people offer such proof."[15]

In all, 20,000 families in four counties left their homes by the orders and might of the Union army, complemented by the state militias and red legs that could cross the border. Decades later, Missouri would still refer to this region as the Burnt District, largely for the destruction that preceded and followed the eviction of suspect Missourians. Shootings and hangings took place throughout the time period; either in homes or on the road, and it was not uncommon to see scenes of executions and corpses from previous murders on the roads. The lucky ones at least could take their belongings, at least for a while; all roads were littered with abandoned possessions like furniture and clothes with greater frequency as one neared the border of Missouri with other states. For those who had no wagons and horses, they could take nothing with them.

---

[15] Schultz, *Quantrill's War*, 243

George Caleb Bingham's painting depicting the carrying out of the orders.

Thomas Ewing, Jr.

Senator Jim Lane

    The effects of General Order No 11 was more profound than the creation of a wasteland. The flood of refugees put pressure on already-impoverished Confederate states, namely Arkansas and eastern Texas, and destitution ensured that the most desperate Missourians began to rob people in other states, targeting Unionist strongholds in northern Arkansas and Texas. Predictably, more refugees emerged, and the roads in the Trans-Mississippi were filled with more homeless, frightened families. This also meant the roads were full of robbers, rogues, and deserters who preyed upon the weak.

Despite these orders, Kansans wanted more revenge upon Missouri, and Lane accused Ewing, who was already hated by a great number of Kansans for the Sack of Lawrence, of not doing nearly enough to prosecute General Orders No. 11. Lane even suggested that he be given an army of 5,000 civilians to invade Missouri. Alarmed at this proposed vigilantism, Union General John Schofield issued General Orders No 92, stating that it was illegal for any armed body of civilians, organized for the purpose of self-defense, to enter another state. Lane may have failed in his attempt to use the destruction of Missouri to further his political career, but he need not have bothered, because by 1864, it was too late. Slavery on the western border of Missouri had collapsed as an economic system due to the damage done by the war.

Quantrill realized that the burned-down crop fields and hollowed-out homes of southern Missouri offered no sanctuary for bushwhackers, so after the massacre of Union soldiers at Baxter Springs, the guerrilla leader left for Texas, one of the few fronts in the Civil War where Confederate troop strength outnumbered the Union. Already beset by refugees of the war, and beseeched by rampant problems of desertion, Texas still represented a chance to hold out as an enclave of the Confederacy; in fact, the state was home to the Missouri Confederate government-in-exile at the town of Marshall. It was hoped by Major General J. Bankhead Magruder, commander of the District of Texas, and Brigadier Henry E. McCulloch, that the epidemic of lawlessness and desertion could be stopped, and they looked to Quantrill to arrest and hang deserters on the roads, curb highway robbery, and destroy liquor stills on the border with the Cherokee Nation, allies of the Confederacy. Not surprisingly, Quantrill refused to do any of this; in fact, his own men participated in the outlaw contingent that infested Texas. Quantrill turned into a major source of irritation for Texas authorities, and he refused to have his men enlist in the regular army per instructions by Magruder. On top of that, when Texas looked to use the irregulars in combat in east Texas at Corpus Christi, Quantrill would not go.

Quantrill realized that inactivity in Texas was slowly dissolving his band, and Cole Younger, one of his best lieutenants, was one of the first to leave. Perhaps recognizing the inevitability of a reduced force and/or trouble with Confederate army regulars in Texas, Quantrill wrote to Governor Reynolds of Confederate Missouri, asking for a commission to invade Missouri. Reynolds advised him to seek a regular commission in the Confederate army for the purposes of rising in fortune and rank, as the role of guerrilla chief usually always ended in two things: becoming a prisoner of the ambitions of the men or facing usurpation by a lieutenant. The lack of a real fight was exactly what caused this to happen. A period of outlaw banditry, drunkenness, and murder saw Bloody Bill Anderson finally leave the band and precipitate a standoff with George Todd, a humiliation that forced Quantrill to leave his force.

While Quantrill's time as a guerrilla captain came to a close, he would continue to bushwhack with Anderson and Todd in a limited capacity during General Price and Major Shelby's calamitous invasion of Missouri in late 1864 -- the Price Raid -- the last Confederate campaign in the West. Anderson and Todd would soon be dead, but Quantrill was able to enjoy some time with his teenage wife. Nevertheless; his desire for fame and fortune would call him again, this time to Kentucky.[16]

Chapter 8: Quantrill's Death

In Kentucky, Quantrill's reputation followed him, but his former success did not. The infamous "Quantrell," as people spelled his name, was known for his crimes against Kansas, so Southern men sang his praises in Kentucky. However, the federal cavalry in the state was much more experienced and successful against guerrillas here, and the end of the war was nearly upon the South. By late 1864, William Tecumseh Sherman was on the march through Georgia, eastern Tennessee had fallen, Robert E. Lee refused to be the Commander in Chief of the Confederate army; and nothing would prevent President Lincoln's reelection.

When asked to write a note for an admirer, Quantrill pilfered the prose of Lord Byron, but the content belonged to him:

"My horse is at the door,
And the enemy I soon may see
But before I go Miss Nannie
Here's a double health to thee.

Here's a sigh to those who love me
And a smile to those who hate
And whatever skies above me
Here's a heart for every fate.

Though the cannons roar around me
Yet it shall still bear me on
Though dark clouds are above me
It hath springs which may be won.

In this verse as with the wine
The libation I would pour
Should he peace with thine and mine
And a health on thee and all in door

Very respectfully your friend

W.C.Q."

---

[16] Report of Maj[or] General Sterling Price: Prices 1864 Missouri Expedition, *Missouri Division: Sons of Confederate Veterans*, http://www.missouridivision-scv.org/pricereport1864raid.htm

The girl would have the poem for 27 years before she presented it to Quantrill's still-grieving mother, who had gone to Missouri and Kentucky to find her disappeared son. What his mother eventually found was the unmarked grave of William Clarke Quantrill, buried at St. Marks Catholic Cemetery in Louisville, Kentucky. Whether or not she heard about the last moments of his life is not known, but she did learn what her son had done in his service to the Southern cause, or more significantly, in his quest for fame.

Quantrill had died on June 6, 1865, shot in the back during a raid in Kentucky that had taken place several weeks after the Civil War had ended. Before long, federal authorities realized who they had captured, so he was moved to the infirmary of a military prison, where he was visited by old colleagues such as Frank James before he died. McCorkle described Quantrill's final days: "He ran to his horse and as he started to mount him, his stirrup leather broke, throwing him across his saddle and, before he could regain his position, his horse dashed out of the door, following the other horses, and just as his horse entered the lot with him, a Federal shot him in the back, the bullet ranging up and forward. His horse ran with him into a pasture. Quantrell still trying to regain his seat and, as the horse made a turn, he fell to the ground on his back and a Federal rode by him, shooting at him when he exclaimed, 'It is useless to shoot me any more; I am now a dying man.' The Federals carried him into Dr. Wakefield's house, where his wounds were dressed and the Federals left him there that night. After the Federals left him, Frank James, John Ross, Bill Hulse and Payne Jones went to see him and wanted to take him away and hide him in the woods, but he declined to go, saying, 'Boys, it is impossible for me to get well, the war is over and I am in reality a dying man, so let me alone. Goodbye,' and the boys turned and left him."

Given last rites as a Catholic, Quantrill died soon after being shot, and newspapers were vague about his identity in his passing. The *Daily Democrat* only spoke of the death of a "guerrilla calling himself William Clark, Captain in the Fourth Missouri rebel cavalry, but generally supposed to be the infamous monster Quantrell." Nearly three decades later, his mother would have Quantrill's bones re-interred for burial in Dover, Ohio. It took longer for his entire body to be buried; the skull was kept by a fraternity at one point before a Dover historical society took possession of it and some of his bones. Fought over by a Confederate cemetery in Missouri, his skull was finally buried in Dover on October 30, 1992. Saluted by men in Confederate uniforms, Quantrill's legacy continued to survive intact, a memory of not just the Civil War but for the lives of people who join war for personal ambitions. As a PBS special put it, "Even after his death, Quantrill and his followers remained almost folk heroes to their supporters in Missouri, and something of this celebrity later rubbed off on several ex-Raiders -- the James brothers, Frank and Jesse, and the Younger brothers, Cole and Jim -- who went on in the late 1860's to apply Quantrill's hit-and-run tactics to bank and train robbery, building on his legacy of bloodshed a mythology of the Western outlaw that remains fixed in the popular imagination."[17]

---

[17] William Clarke Quantrill (PBS - "The West")

Quantrill Reunion, 1920. First Row: Harry Hoffman, _____, [Quantrill Photo], Jesse E. James. Second Row: Morgan Maddox?, George Noland, John W. Williams. Third Row: John Brown?, Jim Campbell, Willis Redman. Standing: Miss Lizzie Wallace.

A reunion of Quantrill's Raiders

Bibliography

Banasik, Michael E., Cavalries of the bush: Quantrill and his men, Press of the Camp Pope Bookshop, 2003.

Castel, Albert E., William Clarke Quantrill, University of Oklahoma Press, 1999, ISBN 0-

8061-3081-4.

Connelley, William Elsey, Quantrill and the border wars, The Torch Press, 1910 (reprinted by Kessinger Publishing, 2004).

Edwards, John N., Noted Guerillas: The Warfare of the Border, St. Louis: Bryan, Brand, & Company, 1877.

Geiger, Mark W. Financial Fraud and Guerrilla Violence in Missouri's Civil War, 1861-1865, Yale University Press, 2010, ISBN 978-0-300-15151-0

Gilmore, Donald L., Civil War on the Missouri-Kansas border, Pelican Publishing, 2006.

Leslie, Edward E., The Devil Knows How to Ride: The True Story of William Clarke Quantrill and his Confederate Raiders, Da Capo Press, 1996, ISBN 0-306-80865-X.

Peterson, Paul R., Quantrill of Missouri: The Making of a Guerrilla Warrior—The Man, the Myth, the Soldier, Cumberland House Publishing, 2003, ISBN 1-58182-359-2.

Peterson, Paul R., Quantrill in Texas: The Forgotten Campaign, Cumberland House Publishing, 2007.

Schultz, Duane, Quantrill's War: The Life and Times of William Clarke Quantrill, 1837–1865, Macmillan Publishing, 1997, ISBN 0-312-16972-8.

Wellman, Paul I., A Dynasty of Western Outlaws, University of Nebraska Press, 1986, ISBN 0-8032-9709-2.